HEALING OUTLOUD

"No Longer Broken"

AUTHOR'S DISCLAIMER

"This book is a true story. It is a collection of stories reflecting my life's journey from childhood into adulthood that all inspired me to become the person I am today. This book was not written or released to hurt, harm, offend, or embarrass anyone in my family, past relationships, or friendships. Sharing my truth is my spiritual assignment to help inspire, empower, and encourage others who may have a similar story. My book is a product of me *NOT* being a victim but a victor.

It was written for the glory of God."

Healing

the process of making or becoming sound or healthy again

Published in The United States of America

Book Development & Editing
Purpose Writers LLC
info@PurposeWriters.Org
www.PurposeWriters.Org

Author's Contact Information
delizatheauthor@gmail.com

For related resources and information on booking the author to speak, please submit request by email.

TABLE OF CONTENTS

DEDICATION   *6*

INTRODUCTION   *7*

ACKNOWLEDGMENTS   *9*

CHAPTER 1: *Childhood Struggles*   *10*

CHAPTER 2: *Ten To Life*   *43*

CHAPTER 3: *Love & Heartbreak*   *75*

CHAPTER 4: *Losing You*   *86*

CHAPTER 5: *Healing Outloud*   *95*

DEDICATION

This book is dedicated to the
broken, hurting, scared little girl I buried over thirty
years ago. To the girl who didn't have
a voice or the power to express her feelings.
This book is dedicated to the little girl who hid from
her own secrets and ran from her own shame.
The girl who didn't see a winner when
she looked in the mirror. It's dedicated to me
because of my strength and willingness to
finally choose myself over everyone else. Because I
finally decided to heal and not to hurt.
I dedicate this book to the little girl who buried her
scars and never wanted to see them again.
The little girl who didn't know that it was okay to
be free This little girl was me.
This book is a reflection of me ministering to her
younger self and letting her know the things she
suffered as a child were not her fault, the things she
experienced in her young adult life were the
manifestation of the pain she kept inside, and that
no longer had to hide or live a life full of pain,
depression, shame, feeling alone, and lost. I
dedicate this book to the little girl who started
fading away as I became the woman God created,
called, and anointed me to be. I dedicate this
memoir to me.

INTRODUCTION

To truly inspire and motivate others to heal, you must first do the work within yourself. Your soul is the first place that needs your full attention. Your process must be embraced privately, but never be afraid to heal *OUTLOUD*.

This memoir is the epitome of my freedom. It is my truth about my journey, my pain, and my breakthrough. It is my story of the sexual abuse, abandonment, violence, fear, and tragedy I have experienced and overcome.

I chose to heal *OUTLOUD* despite the humiliation, heartbreak, shame, and trauma I had to go through from my childhood. I allowed myself to be vulnerable in front of my family, friends, and the entire world in hopes of revealing how important it is to abandon your past and prepare for your future. I was no longer afraid to express, to feel, to heal.

Readers will receive genuine inspiration to acknowledge what they have been through, motivation to receive the help needed to embrace their healing, and my transparency to provoke them to be okay with healing *OUTLOUD*.

This book will encourage readers, both men, and women, to become the best version of themselves. It provides spiritual empowerment to push readers closer to God and far away from what has hindered them from living, learning, and healing.

It is relevant for this generation, where people are lost and killing themselves from the weight of their past and their pain; much needed for individuals who are afraid to heal *OUTLOUD*.

ACKNOWLEDGMENTS

First…...

I must take this time to give God all the praise and glory again! There is no way I could've completed this book without his strength, direction, and peace. Thank you, heavenly father! You are the head of my life and acknowledging you first will always be my top priority. I am nothing without you.

Secondly…...

I must acknowledge two of the most important boys in my life besides God, my amazing children, Tyren & Jamar. My life is and will always be complete because God gave me you two. Everything I do is for you both. Without you two, there's no me. Mommy loves you both so very much; thank you for being my greatest inspiration and motivation to be the woman I have become today.

Lastly…...

I want to personally acknowledge every friend and family member who took the time to support, love, and celebrate me on this life journey. Every season of my life has not been beautiful, but to those who stuck it out with me despite my challenges and fears, thank you! I appreciate you all more than you will ever know. Your compassion and support have been beyond my imagination, and I am truly humbled and grateful.

CHAPTER 1

Childhood Struggles

Sometimes, things are different from what they seem to be as a child. When you're a child, you dream of having things you need and want. You think everything is really supposed to be okay because you have parents who are supposed to always care for you. Your life is supposed to be carefree, with no worries in this world. You should be living life as a free-spirited, outgoing child.

Well, that wasn't the case for me. I grew up having little to nothing. As a little girl, I've always dreamed of my future and life as an adult. I fantasized about being married by 25, having two children, a nice size elegant home, a fantasy car, and a career as a pediatrician because I always loved kids. Their little smiles warmed my heart.

However, for many of us, life can take an unfortunate twist. Things go the total opposite of what you desired them to be. Sudden changes, unfamiliar warfare, and unknown obstacles can cause you to detour from the path you expected; unfortunately, this is what happened to me. Growing up in a small town, Donaldsonville has good and bad perks. Everyone knows everyone, and I hated living there.

Some may ask why, but I don't mind telling you. The people seemed to be so evil and hateful. It was not a tiny town that didn't share unity and love, yet it was a place of confusion, division, and mistreatment.
In my opinion, no child should have been raised in this town. I didn't have much of a choice, though; I was a child. My mother was raising my siblings and I and doing the best she could to take care of us.

She was battling a drug addiction that we were too you to identify, but by the age of eight or nine, I realized that she was definitely struggling with substance abuse and was having a hard time breaking it. I was unfamiliar with drug use, but I wasn't too young to remember what I had heard about it. However, despite her drug addiction, she loved us! Her battle never stopped her from being an amazing mother and striving to provide for us. She has never allowed us to go to bed hungry, dirty, or unsure whether we would eat the next day.

I will forever love and honor her for this. This revealed her strength and will to do good towards us no matter what she was going through. We didn't have much at all; to be honest, most of the children I attended school with were much more fortunate than I was. They wore the finer things and had expensive backpacks, jewelry, and shoes.

Although I was bothered internally, I wore whatever my mother could afford and chose to be grateful.

I remember having to wear hand-me-downs from some of the children at my school. Their parents were my mother's friends, so they would give her what their children couldn't fit in or didn't want anymore. This was very embarrassing because most of the clothes were too small for me as well. The more I wore high-watered pants and shirts with short sleeves that were apparently too small for me, I started to hate my life. I wanted to remain grateful because I knew my mother was doing her best, but our situation needed to change quickly because I was starting to lose hope.

I wanted things to get better so my siblings and I could live a somewhat normal life like other children. Sadly, some of the children didn't realize how blessed they were and used their spare time to make fun of others. They teased, mocked, and laughed at other children who were not as fortunate as they were. They were cruel, and it didn't make things better when I was already feeling low about myself. I handled the teasing as much as possible, but eventually, it affected me badly.

It started to really put me in a very dark head space. I was young, but for some reason, I knew what self-hatred felt like. I was getting a taste of depression, low self-esteem, and anxiety way too soon.

On top of looking and feeling like a misfit, my mother was still strung out on drugs, which made me want to give up on life and die. Her addiction gave the bullies at my school more ammunition to come for me; it got worse every day.

I had to hear children call my mother a "crackhead," "bum," and "junky" almost every day! I didn't care what they saw her as because, in my eyes, she was the world's greatest mom, and I loved her unconditionally, but I still was happy hearing them degrade her. I wasn't a fighter because my mom didn't play that with us, but there was something brewing in my spirit to pop one of them right into their mouth. My mother would always say, "Let them kids say what they want to say about me, and as long as they don't put their hands on you, ignore them. "She didn't understand my anger and frustration with these bullies.

She was an adult who had already experienced school days, so she was mature in this area, but I was just getting started. I wanted to beat them down and make them pay for every insult, criticism, and pain they caused me.

I just knew obedience was better than sacrifice! had I whipped these kids assess, she would've indeed beaten mine. I was not the child who willingly signed up for an ass whipping. My mom was all about us getting good grades, being respectful, and staying out of trouble.

She wanted us to remain in good character regardless of what others did to harm us. I knew better to keep my fist away from their faces because it would only work against me later. My experiences every day were painting a horrible picture of my future. So many things belittled me and caused others to see me as a nobody, a target that deserved mistreatment. I remember one incident that followed me all the way to middle school.

We were in class, and I got up to use the restroom. As I was walking alongside the table, there was a roach crawling. My classmate saw it and yelled, "oh, that roach came out of your pocket"! He and I knew the roach didn't come out of my pocket, yet he insisted on saying it did. That was embarrassing because the kids in my class believed it came from me.

He started calling me roach, and so did everyone else. I just wanted to run and hide. Like really! Why would they think I would carry a roach with me to school, kids, I tell you! After that day, I truly hated that my mom was going through her addiction.

It made things much worse for me, and I really felt like that was the key reason the children continued to torture me. I cried to myself to sleep many nights, praying that God would make her better and improve our situation.

I would ask him to strengthen her to break and shake her addiction, provide better clothes and shoes, and give us stability. I was very tired of living from place to place, struggling, wearing hand-me-downs, and battling bullies. I was TIRED, but I never stopped believing in God, and my faith remained strong.

I knew that God had to be hearing my prayers because there was no way he was going to allow this to continue to happen. Then one day, it was like God truly answered me. I'll never forget this day. After school one day, my mom told me we would be moving away for a while, and someone would help us get our lives together. That was the happiest day of my life.

I was so excited about leaving all those mean and hateful kids behind, and finally, my mom would get some help. I thought about a new place, new people, new friends, and a new start in life as we traveled the highway to our new destination. I didn't know where we were going; I didn't care. All I cared about was getting away from Donaldsonville. She explained that we would temporarily live in a shelter, but I was too young to really understand what a shelter was.

Again, I was happy to be leaving and didn't care. I just wanted to be a normal kid with regular friends that didn't bully me or call me names. Once we arrived, I saw other mothers with their children, just like my mom. They were battling the same issues my mom had, and there was no judgment whatsoever. We all got along very well like one happy family.

Everyone there was so nice and friendly, nothing like the people back home. They actually cared about your well-being and truly wanted to help better our situation. The schools there were nothing like D'ville schools either. The children were much more friendly and didn't care what you wore to school. They didn't bully me either. I wanted to stay in this shelter forever: it was the best thing that happened to us.

However, after living in the shelter for a few months, we returned home, a place I hated so much. We were right back at square one. I didn't want to leave, but I had no choice. When we returned, we first lived with other people, but my mother and stepfather moved us into our own place. We finally had a roof over our heads, our very own.

Boy was I happy, but that didn't last too long! Shortly after finding stability, we were homeless again. Now, don't get it twisted, not all things were wrong with my mom. My mother was a phenomenal woman. She was one of the best aunts her nieces and nephew could have.

She was what you called a real one. In my eyes, she was the world's most incredible mother, and I loved her so much. Despite her addiction, my mother was fantastic, and I could care less if anyone thought differently. I can still remember like it was yesterday before I knew that my mom had an addiction, how she would have the whole house clean, dinner cooked before breakfast was over, and how she had my siblings and I cleaned and dressed, sitting on the couch; ready to start our day. She was very organized and timely with house duties and her motherly duties.

On family park days, we were swinging and sliding like there weren't any struggles in the world. I didn't even know at those exact moments that my mom was struggling with drug addiction. She made struggle look like a blessing. I was extremely attached to my mom. Wherever she went, I was there. I was most definitely her shadow.

I never wanted to be away from her because she really was my everything. When I was about nine years old, I remember my mother leaving my brother and me at one of her friend's houses. At that age, I didn't question any decisions she made. She told us that she was going to the store and would be right back, but she never returned. When she didn't return the first day, I didn't think much about it because it was just the first day.

I've stayed by her friend's house before, so that didn't bother me. But when we reached day four, I got worried. I remember overhearing the woman who owned the house saying, "we need to either call their grandparents or we will have to call the cops. She's been gone too long; these kids need to be with family." All I remember saying was, "please don't send us to foster care."

Please call our grandparents; they will come and get us. "And that's exactly what they did. My brother and I moved in with my grandparents.

At that time, they were only raising our oldest sister, who is two years older than me. Although we were safe and in a stable environment, I still wanted my mother.

I told myself daily that she would be coming back for me. I knew she would; she had to be coming back because she would never leave us like this. My mother would never leave us without an explanation. We hardly even knew our grandparents. Yes, they were family, but they didn't know us like our mother.

I counted as the seconds turned into minutes, minutes turned into hours, hours turned into days, days turned into months, and months turned into years. She NEVER came to take me back with her. It was a few months before she actually returned, only to give my grandparents guardianship over us. Then she was back off to do her own thing. I couldn't believe it!

I was very grateful for my grandparents taking us in because I knew we would have a much more stable home, but I couldn't understand why she didn't talk to me before leaving like that. That really damaged me. I felt abandoned and unwanted by my mother. I knew it was for the better that my grandparents had us, but I needed to understand why my mother did what she did. Unfortunately, I never had the courage to ask her.

I never wanted to be one of the many people to judge her. I loved her regardless of how I felt, so I set aside what I felt, trying to protect her feelings. All of her life, people judged her; I didn't want to become one of those people. I just wanted to let her know how much I loved her regardless. The day she left me was when I started to feel abandoned, and from that day, I've had issues trusting people or allowing anyone into my space.

Her sudden absence damaged my life. It has really affected me mentally and emotionally. I had no idea how to adjust to this change, but I had no choice but to wake up every day and try to conform. It takes time for children and even adults to jump into any change, but some people truly believe adapting to change should happen overnight. This was definitely not working for me.

Living with my grandparents, I tried adjusting as the years passed but couldn't. Being with someone for nine years of your life, then boom, you're living with people you barely know, wasn't easy. I kept telling myself it was for the better. My grandparents were old-school parents. They raised their children the same way they tried to raise us, or rather, me.

As I got older, they became very strict. My oldest sister could do as she pleased, maybe because my grandparents raised her. Things were different for her since birth. She could party, have a boyfriend, and hang out with friends, but I had to go to school, get good grades, and go home, which wasn't bad, but I also wanted a little freedom. I couldn't do half the things my sister was allowed to do.

She was able to get away with literally everything. Even when she and I would get into fights like typical sisters, I would get in trouble. She didn't have to do chores, but I did. They bent backward to make things happen for her. As for me, it was "you get what we give you."

We had a horrible relationship in the beginning. She didn't like me, and hell, I didn't like her ass either. Only because of the way she treated me. Before I moved in with her and my grandparents, we never really knew each other. Since she was the only child with them for the longest, I guess she felt some kind of way, having to share now the two people she had all to herself for years.

A part of me understood how she felt, but the other part of me felt like, no matter what, I'm still your sister; why treat me like I was nothing to you? I hated it. I hated being there!

If this is where we were going to live and grow up as an adult, things would have to get better than this. We used to fight and argue like cats and dogs. But somehow, I was the only one who would get in trouble for it.

I would get called a "black bitch" when I would go against my sister for whatever reason. It was even to the point that I would get told, "I can't stand your black ass," when my sister and I got into it. My sister used to do vindictive shit she knew she could get away with as a way of trying to be in control. She didn't want me there and made me feel hated. No matter what, I had to toughen up and keep it moving to help ease what I was going through.

Despite our love-hate relationship, she loved me, and I loved her. It was a weird kind of love, but it was there. Between the mistreatment and being blamed for everything, my mother's absence also took a huge toll on me. I was already a timid child, but now, I was really starting to shut down even more. I started refusing to express myself and held everything in.

I didn't know how to express my feelings, and no one was teaching me how to. I was hurt; I felt so out of place. I desperately needed to be with my mom. It wasn't about a house, new clothes, or stability at this point. I wanted my mother in whatever condition she was in as long as we were together.

She was my everything, and I missed her like crazy. In my mind, she was coming back to get us, and things would return to normal, but she would only visit and leave us again. After a few years, I chose to suck it up and move forward from the possibility of never living with her again. The reality was I had to stay with my grandparents, so I might as well have gotten used to it. I started to adjust to my new home, neighborhood, and school.

The bullying didn't stop 100% because I was the new girl, but it definitely wasn't what I experienced back in my old hometown. My grandmother could provide better for me, so I remained grateful and decided to live as if I were never going elsewhere again. I didn't make many friends during elementary school, and even when I moved on to middle school, I still didn't have any. A few of my family members attended school with me, but I usually stayed to myself. I didn't talk much; I always just sat back and observed what was happening around me.

I only spoke when spoken to or when it was about class assignments. Other than that, I was in my own zone. Time flew by during the first year of middle school. Over the summer, I had time to think about overcoming my fear of making friends. I knew for sure that I wanted to make new friends during my seventh-grade year.

My goal was to communicate with other children, find my place in the school, and make new friends. I needed to accomplish this no matter what. Although I had difficulty trusting others, especially after being bullied back home, I was ready for the next school year. I was afraid to let people in my personal space, but eventually, I did. At first, I struggled with my new changes, but I improved tremendously as the school year continued.

One of the first things I did was join the school's track team. This was very big and challenging for me because I was terrified of being around groups of people. I was very nervous, but I decided to continue facing my fears and be involved. Running track most definitely took me out of my comfort zone, and I needed to be. Thankfully, one of the girls on the track team made it very easy for me to open up and talk.

She was very friendly; we remained friends after the season was over. Having someone to talk to without being judged or made fun of was major for me. For the first time ever, I felt like I had a true friend. I could tell she was raised in a loving family because of how she spoke and cared about my feelings. Later, that year, I realized I was coming out of my shell.

I began talking to other people more and finding my voice and my own way. I stopped allowing people to speak to me recklessly and began defending myself when someone tried to make fun of me. There were times when I felt my depression kicking in, but I never allowed it to get me back to where people bullied me. When I needed to step away from people to breathe, that's what I did. Things were getting better at school but not home because I still felt like an outcast.

I honestly did because I knew my family didn't want me; I was really only there because I was one of her grandchildren. Something made me uncomfortable, but I just learned to adapt to my new atmosphere. My grandfather and I had a very close relationship. He helped me with a lot of things I needed growing up. When it came down to feeling a parent's love, he was the father I never had.

He taught me about the Bible and how to pray. He was my go-to person for everything; we had each other's back. My grandmother and I had a love-hate relationship because my sister was her favorite. She would go against the world for my sister, providing her with the things she needed and wanted. If it wasn't for my grandfather and a few other people who helped me along the way, I don't think I would have made it.

During my summers off from school, I started going to my aunt's house to help her out because she worked a lot. I would spend my entire summer helping her do things around the house. Sometimes, she would also take me with her to work. While there, she would show me everything she did as a store manager. I would help her with stocking and cleaning once it got close to closing time.

She didn't know that I admired her hard-working skills, and she thrived at being good at what she did; her work ethic was incredible. When she thought I wasn't paying attention, I was. I would stay home with my cousins for most of my other free time. Spending time with them was fun, and we did many things that I wouldn't do back home. I was free to be outside as long as I was in before the streetlights came on. My aunt didn't have a tight grip on me.

She allowed me to be a child. Being there, I made friends with the neighborhood kids, which made being there worth the while. Once summer was over, she would take me school shopping, making sure I had everything I needed to start the school year off right. We did that until I was sixteen, and I started feeling like I didn't want to go out there anymore. I wanted to get a job and take care of myself, and I did.

I was over having to rely on other people to buy for me. I was over having to go to my aunt's house for the summer to help her to get school clothes. Why couldn't I just be taken care of like an average child; instead of committing my summers to cleaning up to get clothes? Don't get me wrong, I'll forever be grateful but let's be honest here; why the hell couldn't I just be taken care of like my sister? She didn't have to do all of that.

She automatically had my grandparents buying her clothes and supporting all that she did; I was the black sheep. However, once I turned sixteen, I started working my first job at Winne Dixie and worked there until my senior year of high school. I was super excited! Finally, I could care for myself when it was time to go school shopping. I wanted to save money to buy whatever I wanted when it was time for school, but people had other plans for my money because I wasn't allowed to hold it myself.

Once my checks were cashed, my grandma gave me what she thought I should get, and the rest was supposedly being saved. When it came down to going school shopping, I had zero dollars and zero cents saved from my checks. So, what I thought I had, I didn't. I was back at square one when it came down to having things for school. Like where did all my money go from my work?

But you can bet one thing; my sister had her shit for school. Could you imagine working and thinking you had money saved only to discover someone else had spent the money? My anger and emotions were all over the place. It was already sad enough that I was working hard for my money to have someone else control what I did with it. I wanted to quit.

But I knew deep inside that I didn't want that to stop me from being independent. I continued to stick it out with the hopes of things changing. The fact that nothing changed bothered me, knowing that I was working hard and not being able to enjoy anything from it. One day I decided to call my nanny because I was tired of going through the foolishness of living in that house. I called her to tell her exactly how I felt about everything.

My nanny meant everything to me, and she was the only one who ever truly listened to what I had to say. She had my back for everything. When she came over to talk to my grandma about my feelings and how it wasn't right to treat me that way, my grandma got mad at me. That night she punched me for calling my nanny. I wanted out of that house badly.

I just couldn't understand why. I thought about why I deserved to be treated the way I was because I'm not a disrespectful child.

I stayed to myself and was not out in the streets fighting or causing trouble at home, so why be nasty towards me? I decided that I didn't want to live there anymore. Living with my Godparents is where I wanted to be, but my grandma refused to let me go live with them.

Without a doubt, I knew that those two people loved me wholeheartedly. They were my favorite people in the world, other than my mom.
The verbal abuse in that home was real. Being called a "bitch," and hearing the words "fuck you" or "I hate you" had become normal to me. I grew numb to those words; my heart grew colder and colder by the day.

By that time, I was past my breaking point. My main focus was to finish school and graduate. Getting away from that toxic bullshit was my number one priority. To help pass my time and stay there, I began to keep myself busy with sports and dancing. The more active I was, the less time I spent in that house.

Playing sports and dancing required after-school practice during the week, which meant late days getting home. Some days after school, I would go straight to work. All that helped me with balancing myself once I got home.

I recall our baby brother being at my grandparents' house to stay for the weekend on time, and our oldest sister started a big commotion with him. She wanted to whoop him with a belt, and I wasn't having that at all.

My brother and I had been through so much together, so there was no way she would put her hands on him. We were all in there fussing and fighting. My sister had hit me on my elbow with an air freshener can, and we both started fighting again. Out of everyone fighting, my grandmother came straight for me and slapped me across my face, causing my eyeglasses to fly across the room. At that moment, I lost all the common sense I had.

All of my built-up anger and frustration had come out. I began screaming in her face telling her how much I hated her, I didn't want to be there, and that she was an old evil bitch. She tried to hit me again, but by that time, my grandfather had made it into the living room to tell her not to hit me again. I broke out the front door to leave. She tried chasing me but fell down the steps outside.

As I watched her fall, I shouted to her, "I hate you, I'm leaving, and I am never coming back to this evil house." I ran that night in the rain barefoot all the way to my aunt's house. It seemed like I was running forever.

I was soaking wet when I got to my aunt's house, and my feet were cold. She told me to dry myself off and that she would handle it in the morning.

After that night, I was in between homes. Some days, I was at my aunt's, and others back at my grandparents. I eventually ended up back over there altogether. Yup, I still had to return to a place I didn't want to be; I had no choice but to go. Graduating high school was still my number one priority.

I was willing to humble myself all the way until I got the hell out of that house, but they knew better not to keep trying me the way they did. I was ready for whatever and whoever! After that night, I learned how to stand up for myself. I was finally okay with letting my family know they couldn't treat me any way, thinking it was okay to do so. They needed to know that I had feelings too.

The drama nor foolishness stopped there because life continued to throw curveballs. I ended up running away from home again, but it was not to a family member this time. The guy I was dating at the time came and picked me up. I returned to his mom's house to stay with him for about a week. Of course, I knew that I couldn't stay there full-time because I was still a minor, and his mom said she would call my family and tell them where I was eventually.

The next day I left and went to my aunt on my dad's side. I knew that her spot was the only place I could stay. I stayed there for about three nights and went home after talking to my nanny. She promised to come and get me the next day and she did. This time my grandmother didn't fight to keep me there, so she allowed me to pack my clothes and leave with my nanny.

All I wanted from the beginning was to be with someone who truly loved me. None of my friends at school knew what I was going through besides my guy best friend, who knew just about everything about me. Living with my godparents was so much better. I had a breath of fresh air. She taught me the meaning of life and all the lessons that came with it.

I was in a happy place. Those two people led me to stand firm when all odds were against me and never to fold under any pressure. She applied God in our lives daily, keeping me grounded and rooted to believe in the God we served. She drove me to school every day until she taught me how to drive. She's the one who gave me my first driving lesson when she put me behind the wheel of her car and said, "drive me."

I had never driven a car, but I always paid attention when I rode in the front seat to how a person turned the wheel in the direction they wanted to go in and what each letter did; I knew the basics of winging it. My nanny was the first to allow me to date a boy openly. We had that open relationship where I could talk to her about anything. While living with them, I continued striving for what I wanted, and once I walked across that stage, I knew all the foolishness I had gone through was over. I knew that no one would or could ever hurt me again.

I was all over the place my entire life with absolutely no stability at all. I bounced from home to home or to whoever felt they wanted to be bothered at the time until I moved with my Godparents. I've seen a lot starting from my early childhood days. I was shifting into a young adult, but my heart was still holding on to painful things that caused me so much anger, unforgiveness, and rage. Life experiences broke me from a very young age.

I went from battle to battle, war to war, pain to pain. Many wondered what the root of my rage was but never seemed to care to ask or provide the counseling and love I needed to heal, forgive, and grow. I mean, did these people know what I had to go through? Did they even care?

I watched my mother struggle with drug addiction, was introduced to poverty, and the struggle long before I knew what it was, and I witnessed my mother overdose.

I was bullied in school by peers I should've been playing with and harshly mistreated by my blood sister and grandmother. Not to mention the terrifying sexual abuse I suffered, first by a family member and then by a young man who was my mother's friend's son. No one ever asked why I had so much built-up frustration and anger inside me, but if they had taken a second, a minute, or an hour to talk to me, they would have known what I had suffered. Instead, they shut me out, and you learn to keep things to yourself when you don't have anyone to confide in and trust. My family swept so many things under the rug that I knew that if I told, no one would believe me.

I would have been cursed out, whooped, or called a liar. I could've told my nanny but moving with her was the beginning of my happy place. I wanted to put everything I had been through behind me and live as if it had never happened. I was completely unaware of how important it was to talk about and release it. In my mind, it was over, and I was in my new place to start over.

There was no reason for me to revisit my pain when it was supposed to be over. Besides, opening up with anyone about your sexual abuse to anyone is very difficult. It's embarrassing, painful, and shameful, especially when another family member first did it. I just wanted peace and to be an average young adult; that's what I focused on each day afterward. After being sexually assaulted, the visuals never go away.

It's like the scene is stuck on replay; that's why some of us can remember what has happened to us so clearly. The first assault happened before I moved with my grandparents. One day, my mother and her friend went out to have fun, leaving me, my brother, and her kids, who we considered our cousins' home, with her nephew. He was old enough to stay home with us, and we were excited not to have our parents around. We knew that we could play all night and then clean up before they made it back home.

We jumped from couch to couch, running, hiding, and throwing pillows all over the place. I remember running from the boy watching us; I would jump on the couch so that he couldn't catch me, and I would be safe. The couch was our base; once we reached it, you wouldn't be IT, or that person couldn't touch you because you would technically be considered safe. He wasn't playing fair because he pulled me off the couch by my legs, causing my head to hit the floor.

When he did that, I felt a rush instantly to my head that wouldn't stop throbbing.

It felt as though I had a heartbeat in my head. I began to cry historically and didn't want to play anymore. I got off the floor and ran into the bedroom, crying and screaming that I would tell my momma when she returned. My brother and cousins came to check on me, but I didn't want to be bothered by anyone; I just wanted to be left alone. I cried for what seemed like forever before he came into the room, saying that he was sorry and that he didn't mean to hurt me.

I remember screaming at him, "Get away from me and leave me the heck alone." I was lying in bed with my face smothered in the pillow when he came and climbed into the bed with me. His apologetic demeanor when he said he was sorry had gone out the window the moment he lay next to me. He told me to "shut up" while he grabbed me, turning me on my back. My heart began to skip beats instantly as he climbed on top of me.

I began to scream for him to get off me while trying to fight him off, but he covered my mouth with his hands as he continued to tell me to shut it and to stop fighting him. My screams became muffled, but I continued screaming, kicking, and fighting for him to get off.

With one hand over my mouth and the other touching and feeling all over my body, he somehow put my legs between his legs so I could no longer kick him. He touched every part of my body with his bare hands before attempting to pull his pants down but couldn't because he needed both hands. While lying there, the tears continued to fall, and all I could do was wish my mom was there to save me.

Once he realized he couldn't unbuckle with one hand, he uncovered my mouth. I began to scream all over again for my brother and cousins to come and help me. They began to beat on the bedroom door for him to open it, but he yelled for them to go away from the door. I knew that he would rape me and that there was nothing anyone could do to stop him. Somehow, they were able to get into the room.

They were all screaming, telling him to stop and to get off me. This time he listened and stopped trying to rape me, getting up to fix his clothing as if nothing had ever happened. My brother ran and shouted that he was going to tell our mom. I was afraid of what would happen when my mom found out what he did. My mind kept telling me that she would kill him and be in jail for the rest of her life.

I mean, that's what I thought most parents would do for their kids in situations like this. I was way too young to understand why this was happening to me.

Why would anyone want to hurt me in that manner? Unfortunately, he didn't stick around to find out what would happen to him when my mom made it back because he left us in the house after he sexually assaulted me. I stayed up all night waiting for my mother to come home.

It was very late, almost the next day, and to my surprise, she didn't show up until the sun had risen. I woke up to my brother's voice telling my mom what had happened. My eyes met her eyes; without any words, it was like she was speaking to me through them. I didn't say anything to her; I just stared in complete silence. She then shouted for me to get up and put my shoes on so we could go, never addressing the issue or talking to me about what had happened to me.

My brother was much younger than me, so maybe she thought he didn't know what he was talking about, but if looks could kill, I would have been dead. As we walked alongside the road, I remember her saying to my brother, "let me find out you're lying. I'm going to whoop your ass." Both my brother and I knew that he wasn't lying about anything. I was quiet for a while, but I finally had the courage to tell her that my brother was telling the truth and the boy had touched me all over my body.

My mom didn't say anything back to me; she just once again looked at me as if she wanted me to shut my mouth, so I did. I didn't utter another word. As we made it to our destination, my mom began to talk to the boy's mother. Back in the day, when adults were talking, kids weren't allowed to be in their conversation, so my brother and I played in the parking lot. Once my mom got off the phone, I never heard anything else about the situation.

Not once did my mom ever talk to me about what I experienced. She never sat me down to even explain anything to me. At that moment, I truly believed that my mom didn't believe anything my brother and I had said. Why didn't she believe me? Why didn't she protect me from this pervert?

How many other kids had he done this to? All kinds of things ran through my head, and at that very moment, my brother and I promised always to protect one another from any and everybody because we were all we had. If we didn't protect each other, who would? Just like that, my assaulter was still free to roam the streets, and my abuse was swept under the rug. It was hidden away as a deep dark secret between my mom and his family.

Even though other kids saw with their own eyes, nothing was done about it. This triggered something inside me at a very young age causing me not to trust people. Even though I loved my mom, I couldn't trust her to protect me anymore. I tucked what happened to me in the back of my mind and tried to forget about it. It never went away!

The sexual assault happened to me a second time by my uncle; I was a preteen. It caused that little girl once sexually assaulted to resurface, forcing me to drift back down memory lane to what had happened to me before. I was back in that same situation, just with a different person. I was sexually assaulted by a man I had been around for years. I never thought once that he would do something like that to me, but I guess it was more of how a hawk watches its prey before making a move.

He had watched me grow up from a little girl into a pre-teen, so my thoughts were how could, how could he? He would never try to penetrate me, only forcing himself to kiss me on the lips and sticking his hands down my shirt to touch my breast. Fighting him off each time became a routine. It was as though he knew the perfect time to come around and make his move. The smell of his breath, the touch of his lips against mine, and his hands on my breast made me sick to my stomach.

It made my skin crawl. I am not sure how many other family members he had done this to, but I guess it was my turn. By then, I had heard so many horrible family secrets that I was too afraid to tell anyone what was happening. Every family secret always came out during family arguments. It was as if when someone got mad, that was always the day a new family secret of how a family member molested one, but nothing was ever done about it.

So, when I started being touched, I already knew that no one would believe me and that, once again, it would be another painful secret swept underneath our family rug. Hell, when it happened the first time, my own mother didn't believe my brother or me. Therefore, I kept it all to myself, not telling a soul about what was happening. I honestly felt that no one would care or believe me if I told them. Why should they?

No actions had ever been taken from the previous attack that had taken place in my family, so what would have made this one any different? It would become another family topic to discuss during toxic conversations or gossip. Eventually, I grew numb to life and all the things that came with living. That's when I began having suicidal thoughts about taking my own life. I had gotten to where I thought I would be better off dead.

I thought about many ways to end my life, but I always heard my grandfather's voice loudly saying, "God doesn't forgive those who kill themselves, and you won't make it into heaven." Hearing those words kept me many times from ending my own life. Also, my love for my siblings wouldn't allow me to do it either. I couldn't stomach how they would feel if something happened to me. All I knew was that I couldn't understand why I had to go through so much at such a young age.

I was trying to figure out what I did wrong to deserve what happened to me, only to realize that I didn't do anything wrong, and it wasn't my fault. The curses never broken over my family life were triggering down over my life. The more I went to church, the more I understood that I was the oil carrier and had an anointing on my life that the devil didn't like. He was trying to destroy me in every way possible, but the God I serve wouldn't allow him to possess my life. I kept praying and believing that God would turn my situation around, and he did just that.

I began to pray for those who hurt me throughout my life. What the devil meant for evil, God turned it for my good. What was meant to break me made me stronger. God didn't allow my experiences to make me bitter; he used them all to make me better. I was forced to heal *OUTLOUD*.

CHAPTER 2

Ten To Life

I will never forget April 1, 2007; it was a day that changed my life. Let me take you on a journey down a memory of that. It will tell you how I ended up in this situation. In 2005, I met a guy through one of my close friends. He was her cousin, an evacuee that had recently moved to Donaldsonville due to Hurricane Katrina.

He was a very nice young man who came from a great family. After our introduction, he and I started conversing, and a few months later, we decided to give it a shot at a relationship. We welcomed each other into our families and our lives. When we first met, I already had a son who was four months at the time. That wasn't a problem; he and his parents accepted my sons as their own child and grandchild.

The love and kindness they showed the both of us was incredible. The more we dated, the closer we eventually became. They loved us, and we loved them wholeheartedly. My son's biological father wasn't in the picture as much as he should have been, but that caused the guy I was with to have an even closer bond with my son.

He was there every step of the way for my son; through the good and the bad, he was there.

I initially lived with a cousin in a town called White Castle, but my son and I would spend a lot of time with him and his family. I remember receiving a call from my cousin one day, and she told me that she and her family were moving to Atlanta and that I needed to figure out what I would do. I didn't have my own place, couldn't go to any family members at the time, and didn't want to take my son to Atlanta; I just didn't. I remember waking him up to tell him all that was happening, not knowing what to do. Later that day, I told his parents the situation, and they agreed to let my son and me live with them.

I didn't want to overstay my welcome, so I found a job to start saving to get a place. Everything between us was great in the beginning. We did many family things together, but they say you never really know someone until you start living with them. It seemed like everything he was doing started coming to light. I found out he was still talking to old ex-girlfriends and other females, just doing the most.

We started to argue and disagree a lot more than usual. Every day he stayed out late, taking late phone calls, and even on some weekends, he would leave me at the house with his family and leave.

One day I caught him with two girls in the house while I was getting ready for work. At that moment, I knew it was over, and I had to find another place to live quickly. I had to accept it because I lived in his house; who was I to tell him what to do?

I felt hurt, angry, and betrayed! Some nights I would cry, trying to figure out the problem between us. I realized that my life was too much for him. I did have a child when we met, but he already knew that. I eventually got tired and told him I was done.

Months went by with the same thing happening, except now we were not together, and I just lived there. He was free to do whatever he wanted to do. I didn't care anymore. Females called the house all night long looking for him, but I didn't care; I just was at a place where I wanted out! I remember my aunt calling me one day to ask if I wanted to go out of state to work, and I immediately said yes.

I talked to his mom about watching my son so I could work and get my own spot, and she told me they would watch after him while I was gone. I told her I would be gone for about 2-3 months to work in Memphis, but I was definitely coming back to get my son. Leaving my son was the hardest thing that I had to do. We had never been away from each other since he was born, but I knew I had to leave to get our place. It was going to put us in a better place.

I left for Memphis the week after being offered the job. I stayed out there working and saved enough to get a place. While working out there, the guy and I ended up talking about getting back together and making it work, but before we got back together, I told him I would not tolerate his cheating or any other bullshit that would eventually hurt me, my son, or our relationship. He assured me he was done with everything and wanted his family back. I returned home after work just before my son celebrated his first birthday.

We did it together as a family, but after celebrating his birthday, we moved to a new place together, but it was mine. I finally had a new job with a stable income, and I refused to be in another situation where I lived with someone and had to leave when it didn't work out. We were finally in our place of peace - or so I thought. I thought all the bullshit with the other women was over, but boy was I wrong; it seemed like it was just getting started. While working in Memphis, it was clear that he had been dealing with another female.

To make matters worse, she claimed to be pregnant with his child. I couldn't win for losing with this guy, but I didn't let it bother me too much. I know the females from Dville could be messy without reason.

He and I talked about the situation, and he didn't deny messing around with the chick, but he did deny getting her pregnant. He stated, "I had sex with her, but we used a condom, so if she is pregnant, it isn't mine."

I don't remember saying much that day. Two days later, I told him that if she were pregnant, he would need a DNA test and that if the baby were his, he would have to take care of his responsibility. He must stand like a man and take care of what was his if it was his. We both agreed that we would work through it together. I had to understand that this situation happened when he and I weren't together.

However, women become bitter when things don't turn out their way, which causes the other chick to be mad at me. She expected me to be angry with him and break up, but we did the total opposite. We stood firm together. We were happy again, and I honestly wasn't mad with either of them. Once she saw I was unbothered, she threatened me, saying that she and her friends were going to "beat me so bad that my family wasn't going to be able to recognize me."

I tried my best to ignore the threats. As long as they didn't put their hands on me, I didn't care what they said. They had to show me better than what they could tell me.

I was never humbugging, but don't get it twisted; I was with the shits. By all means necessary, I was going to protect myself.

She and her friends started showing up at my job, and that's where I drew the line of allowing her to continue playing with me. I eventually spoke with her mother to inform her of what was happening with her daughter. She didn't say much except that her daughter was grown and couldn't tell her what to do, but she would talk to her about it because she didn't raise her like that. After that conversation with her mom, things died down for a while. The harassment stopped, and the threats ceased for about a month.

Shortly after, things went back to the same as before: threats and all the other foolishness. After a rough workday and a run-around from the insurance company, I returned home to relax. As I pulled up to my driveway, I saw the girl talking to my brother. The threats made to be replayed over and over in my head when I saw her. Not only that, but to my surprise, she wasn't pregnant; I was furious!

I was angry all over again. I told my brother to ask her to leave out of my yard because we didn't get alone and that I had a restraining order on her not to be within 100 feet of me. You think she would have left, right? NOT! She was bold and biggity, saying, "Bitch I'm not going anywhere.

If you want me moved, move me!" That was it. I had lost it! I pushed her in front of my door, and we began to fight. Full of anger, all I saw was red.

I remember grabbing her by the shirt and punching her in the face. I kept hitting her repeatedly until I saw blood coming from her nose and lip. I was clawing my nails into her face, not wanting to let her go, and hearing her screaming for me to stop caused me to hit her more. I kept telling her, "No bitch, this is what your ass wanted, so you will take this ass whooping like a woman. My cousin's girlfriend tried to stop me, but it was too late.

My anger had taken over. I had so much rage and anger built up towards this girl that I didn't even realize my strength or that I beat her up that badly, but honestly, I really didn't care. I WAS READY FOR WHATEVER WHENEVER! After the fight, I called my aunt and grandparents to come and get my child; I just knew I was about to go to jail. Thankfully, that night I didn't go to jail.

The only thing that saved me from not going was the restraining order I had in place and the fact that she was on my premises. That night I reacted without thinking. I knew that the fight was severe. I wasn't trying to hurt anyone; I was angry and fed up.

I've never been the type to go around fighting people, but if you step at me wrong or play with me, I was definitely about that life.

About a month passed, and I didn't hear from or see her. I thought to myself, "okay, finally, this situation with this chick is over with; she's not pregnant, so we can finally put all the BS to rest. She can finally leave me alone." Wouldn't you think so? Wrong!

That fight between her and me only triggered things even more. Only this time, her family got involved. They wanted revenge one way or another. On Easter Sunday, April 2017, my son and I were supposed to stay home. I didn't have any plans to do anything or go anywhere, for that matter.

It was just another day for me, so leaving my home wasn't a big deal. My aunt called and asked if I was coming over because she was having a gathering at her house. I was hesitant about going at first, but then I agreed. Why not? My family was there, so I could get up and go, and I went.

After eating and laughing with family, my cousins and I went for a ride with our kids. Riding through the projects and crossing the bayou on holidays is common in Donaldsonville. That's what we do.

Well, what we thought would be a fun ride turned into a ride from hell. That day changed my life in so many ways.

As we were riding, traffic was bumper to bumper; you couldn't even move. People had gotten out of their cars, dancing, laughing, and talking, but we were still inside our vehicle. Little did we know that the traffic came to a standstill right in front of the girls' family house. They were all outside gathered together celebrating easter with their family. She and I locked eyes immediately, and in my mind, I was saying, "well, I'll be damned."

But of course, I didn't think anything of it because, as I stated before, I thought we squashed the issues. Not at all. The shit was about to hit the fan. Once she noticed I was in the car, she whispered something to one of her family members, and from there, it was on. Before they could approach us, I had already told my cousins I saw her, and I think it was about to be some shit.

Mind you; it was me, my two cousins, and our kids in the car. I honestly didn't want a fight to break out because our kids were in the car, but it was over once they approached the car, beating on the windows and pulling on the door handles. One of my cousins got out of the car, and from there, we all got out.

Before you knew it, we were going up against her family members. The crazy thing about it is I would have fought her again in front of her family, but this time it was different; she and I didn't fight.

I was up against her dad and mom. In my mind, all I could think about was protecting the kids in the back seat. She and her family had surrounded the car. They even tried to get in from the side where the kids were, which sent me into a rage. I wanted to beat the shit out of her all over again. Out of nowhere, her dad punched me on the side of my face, causing a ringing in my ear.

I was barely able to hear. He had me pinned inside the car door where I couldn't move. Then her mom came across her husband's shoulder and punched me in the mouth. My bottom lip was split down the middle, my right ear was ringing, and my face had quickly swollen. At that moment, tears started to fall.

All I could do was beg them not to do anything to cause harm to my child or the other baby in the car. I remember begging them to let us go home to drop the kids off, and I assured them that we would finish what they had started. Her dad then let me go and pulled his wife back. I was LIVID! Somebody was going to pay; I knew exactly who it was.

At that moment, all I saw was death! I felt so much evil flood my spirit, and I wanted her dad to die one way or another because he would have to feel my pain. I didn't want anyone to deal with him other than me. I dropped my son off at my grandma's house, and I wasn't thinking clearly at all. My cousin dropped me off at home to change my clothes, and we were indeed going back to finish what they had started.

While on our way back over there, I immediately got this nauseous feeling in the pits of my stomach. I started feeling like we shouldn't go back, but my family had already returned by then. Apart from my regret of going back over there, the other part of me felt like it was too late to turn around. Everything I wanted to happen to her dad happened. I was still angry and upset, so I didn't care much whether he lived or died.

Things happened so quickly that we didn't even think about what would happen after returning there. Things escalated so quickly between my brother and her dad that no one had a chance to stop to think things through or talk them out like adults. All I heard were screams coming from everywhere. I remember looking back and seeing her dad lying on the ground. I wasn't sure whether he was dead or not, but did I care at the time?

NO! In my mind, I thought that's what he gets from putting his hands on a female. My brother has always been the over-protective one of his sisters, but not in a million years would I have thought that things would happen this way. Once we noticed him lying flat on the ground, we all left. My emotions were all over the place once things were over.

No matter how much my mouth said about wanting him to feel my pain, that wasn't who I was at heart. I had never done anything to hurt anyone, yet I didn't understand how he could hurt me the way he did and did not consider the consequences. When your anger flares up, you don't think straight. Neither party thought clearly that day, and we acted on our emotions. I couldn't sleep that night, and my anxiety was through the roof because I knew the man was dead and we were going to jail.

I felt like everyone was in that situation due to me. If I hadn't fought the girl a few months prior, we wouldn't be at the place we were. That night of the accident, I remember crying my eyes out to my brother for having him in the situation. He was so young and innocent with his whole life ahead of him. I never wanted him to fight my battles for me.

I only wanted what was best for him and felt he would be taken away because of me. We talked about turning himself in and what would happen from there. The next day my grandfather went with my brother to turn himself in. My heart shattered into so many pieces. My baby brother endured so much with me, and now he was going to jail for attempted murder; AND IT WAS MY FAULT!

I was so stressed because I didn't know what to expect after that. I couldn't eat or sleep, and I don't even think I showered because I couldn't function straight. I just wanted him to be safe in jail. Everyone was disturbed. My mind was racing, and I didn't know whether or not everyone would go to jail.

I knew I needed someone to care for my son if anything happened to me; that night, I just held him tight and cried. I apologized in advance if I had to leave him. My son was one and a half at the time. His second birthday was only a month away. I never thought that I would be spending it behind bars.

Days had gone by; I was finally able to pull myself together. I got up one morning, ready for the day when there was a knock on the door. My heart instantly dropped when I heard Donaldsonville sheriff's office. At that moment, I knew the time had come to where I was going to jail.

I kissed my baby for what I thought would be the last time as the tears rolled from my eyes.

So innocent and sweet, he kissed me back, not really understanding what was happening. The officer then read my rights and placed me in the back of the police car. I'd never been arrested a day in my life. I was never a problem child, so this was new. The officers took me into the interrogation room, where they continued to drill me for what seemed to be hours. They tried to throw crosses at me, but all I knew was to say that I didn't want to talk without my lawyer being present. Hell, I learned that from watching so many television shows. It seems crazy, but after I said that the questions stopped. I was then booked into jail on a principal to attempted murder charge. When the lady told me this, it felt like all of the breath I had left in my body left.

I was numb. Never in a million years would I have thought I'd be in jail for a murder charge. No matter how tough I thought I was, I wasn't built for prison. I had a son who needed me to continue to be his mom. What was my child going to do without me?

What was I going to do without my son? He was all that I had. Everything replayed in my head on how I should have handled things. I wished I could take back what had happened, but it was too late. Little did I know, my cousins were in there as well.

They picked them up right before picking me up, and we all were in there on the same charge. All my life, I heard horror stories about what happened to people in jail. I was scared out of my mind, but I knew I couldn't let my fear show. It was either you sink or swim in prison. I decided I needed to stand firm if I wanted to make it in there.

The crazy thing is that everyone in jail was way older than me. The prisoners asked why I was in there, and I told them. They were very encouraging, telling me "To stay strong" and "I would be okay." That was all fine and dandy, but I still wanted to go home to my child. I didn't want to be in there; I knew nothing I could do about it.

I was charged with an attempted murder charge, and they set my bond at half a million dollars. It was no way my family had that kind of money. It went from being one in jail to having four of us in there. My brother didn't have a bond, but my cousins and I did. Many people said the judge was trying to make an example out of us, but I wasn't trying to hear all that; I just wanted out.

As the days went by, I felt like I was dying inside. I missed my son so much. So many things were running through my mind: was he being properly cared for? Did he miss me? Did he cry for me at night? I wanted and needed to know these things.

I was lost and completely unaware of how a jail system works, and I had to wait to be appointed a lawyer. Once I was assigned my lawyer, he ensured I knew everything about the case and what direction we needed to go in to get out. He stayed on top of everything. I recall asking him how much time I could face if the judge found me guilty of the charge. He explained that the charge could carry a ten to a life sentence if found guilty.

The longest they could hold me was ninety days without proof of anything. He kept trying to assure me that I would be home back to my child and that I just had to trust him. After hearing that timeframe, I don't think I could remember another word he said. All I thought about was my baby. I became so numb to the pain of being in there to where I just cried silently inside.

The situation broke my heart, but at this point, I had to trust him if I ever wanted to see freedom again. If only I could have turned back the hands of time to avoid everything I was going through. Before being arrested, I asked his mom to promise to care for my son while I was away. Of course, she said yes. Everyone knew that my son wasn't her biological grandchild and that she loved him like he was her own.

I was curious to know how my son was doing other than word of mouth from her. One thing I knew for sure was that he would be cared for unconditionally. When I was able to call home, I heard his little voice. I missed him daily, wondering if he would still remember me as mom or if he had forgotten about me. Every night I prayed to be able to dream about him and those big eyes he had.

An entire month passed, and I still was behind those iron bars. My son's birthday was approaching- I was losing my mind. Never did I imagine being away from my son for his second birthday. When I called home to speak with him, she told me he was with my family—confused about why they let him leave. She said, "I let him go with your family to keep down confusion."

Trying to understand why they would even try to start confusion when I gave her permission to keep him. Behind a jail cell, I couldn't do much about anything. Not knowing my son's condition and how he was doing caused me to be angry that entire day. While there, I lost my job and my home. Everything I worked hard to accomplish for my son and me was gone within a blink of an eye.

To make matters worse, I was in the situation in the first place because the guy I was dating allegedly made a baby with the chick. None of this would have ever happened if he had not been with her. Or so I thought. I was in jail behind the bullshit he put us through while he was still out free, roaming the streets. There was so much family betrayal while I was locked up.

I was having family steal from me while behind bars; it was a hurtful feeling. The last thing they could have done was make sure they cared for my son while I was gone, but they couldn't even do that because it was about a dollar. Locked up behind bars with little to nothing was awful. I didn't say much, though; I just sat back and observed a lot of foul shit. I knew more than they thought I knew.

While there, I learned how to humble myself and let God fight my battles. What they thought was meant to break me only built me up while lying on that hard mat. My main and only focus was to get out to get my son. I'll forever be grateful for my aunt and cousin, who took my son in as their own. They held my son down while I was locked up.

After they saw how he was being treated and cared for, they took him. As a woman and mother, I had so much respect for them. My cousin didn't have any kids at the time.

It wasn't her responsibility to raise my son, but she did. She didn't know how long I would be away, so she didn't ask. I knew they would care for him and ensure he received the love and attention he needed.

His father was nowhere to be found. He could care less if I got life in jail. If he didn't have to take his son, he would be fine. As time continued to move in slow motion, I became more depressed. Going back and forth before the judge only to keep having the court dates pushed back to a later time, I grew tired and wanted to give up on life.

At night I thought about killing myself, thinking I'd rather be dead than spend the rest of my life behind bars. I felt like God was teaching me a lesson. The only thing that kept me going was my son, who needed me, but that didn't stop me from being fed up. I knew he needed me, but I was tired. One day after coming back from court, I got the biggest surprise of my life.

My mom was there in jail. Yes, my mom, lol. The funny thing about it is my mom was a straight gangster with it. It felt like an enormous weight was lifted off my shoulders when I saw her. No longer did I feel alone.

They didn't have her in the same pod as me, but she was with my cousins. Just knowing that she was there gave me a sense of peace. We only got to hang around each other when we had time to go to the courtyard. I was allowed to hug her for the first time once we made it outside. Hell, I think we all felt safe since she was there. Before my mom got arrested, I had heard so many stories about my mom from the other women in jail, which was hilarious.

It was crazy how they all knew her. No one had anything bad to say about her; they spoke highly of her. Everyone knew her from singing all day. She had such a beautiful voice that would send chills through your body when she sang. No one ever crossed me wrong in there because everyone spoke about how they knew my mom.

It was more like they protected me because they knew her. Most of the women were in there for a murder they committed themselves. I was scared shitless. Those women were real-life thugs, but some truly had a heart of gold. Once I got to know them for myself, I understood them better.

Having people to talk to while locked up made the days a little easier. Every last one of them spoke about how jail wasn't for me and that they never wanted to see me in there again. They didn't have to tell me twice.

I knew that if/when I got out, nothing in the world would ever send me back to that place. I am now two months being in jail, and my anxiety and depression set in.

I didn't know if I was going or coming, but I knew I had to continue not showing it. Silently crying myself to sleep at night had become my routine. I was praying to ask God to touch the judge's heart to allow me to go home. My court date for June had finally come around. I just knew that the judge would let me go home; boy, was I wrong.

Not only did he not allow me to go home, but he rejected the offer of reducing my bond from a half million dollars. Why was the judge being so hard? Was he truly going to keep me in jail for the rest of my life? Will I ever get to hold and kiss my son ever again? These questions constantly replayed in my head.

I was a first-time offender, so why did I have to go through all of this? After being denied a bond reduction, my lawyer spoke with me, saying not to give up and continue to have faith that he would do everything in his power to get me home. I started losing faith in my lawyer, myself, and God. I was almost to a place where I would throw in the towel and say screw it. But that little voice in my head said to continue to have faith the size of a mustard seed.

You will be okay; you will go home. July had approached, and I was still in jail. By then, I was three months in and was basically like, okay, it is what it is. Bond is still high as hell. The lawyer is still saying hold on.

I was over it all. I didn't care anymore what was going to happen. I was going to be there a while, so I might as well get settled in myself. I remember having court around the second week in July. When I got there, in my head, all I kept saying was that the judge would just reset the court date and have me go back again; well, I was wrong.

God had answered my prayers. The judge finally dropped the bond from five hundred thousand dollars to a little nothing. Not only that, my ninety days were up. They couldn't hold me any longer because they didn't have enough evidence to keep me there. I was over-excited with joy and couldn't wait to get home to my son.

Just when I thought everything was good to go, BOOM, a minor setback. My bond was set to where I only had to pay thirteen hundred dollars and some change to get out. For me, that was a roadblock. Where was I going to get that money? I didn't have anyone that could give me that kind of money.

My family barely had my back while I was there with the commissary, so I stood a poor chance of getting that kind of money. Once I got the news about my bond reduction, I called my boyfriend's parents to let them know what was happening. They had been by my side throughout the process, so I had to call them to let them know I'd be home soon. I also explained to them about the money situation, not because I wanted them to pay but to let them know that it was the only thing standing in my way of getting home. His mom and I talked about everything.

I never hid anything from her. We were like an open book around each other. After we finished talking for that day, we said our I love you's and that was the end. Still trying to figure out how I would get that money to get him, I continued to wait patiently until, one day, I called home, and they told me that they had the cash to get me out. His parents had taken the money to the jail to get me out.

I was overwhelmed with joy and excitement. I wasn't expecting them to give me that kind of money, but they did so that I could get home to my child. Being jobless and not having money saved up, I didn't know how to repay them; but I knew I had to. They never asked for it back, but being who I am, I didn't want anything from anyone for free.

They refused to take anything from me but only wanted me to come home and take care of my child as I did before leaving him.

Hearing my name called to go home was the best thing to happen to me. I promised myself that I would never allow anyone to get me out of character again unless my life truly depended upon it.
Once those doors opened to that jail cell and closed behind me, I could only smile. As I walked out of that building, my heart skipped beats. Was this truly happening?

In my head, I kept asking myself, was I actually going home to my son? All I wanted was to hold, kiss, smell, and love on my child. Everything and everyone else had to wait. I was extremely nervous to see my son after being gone for three long months, not knowing how he would react to seeing my face again. Little did I know that he was attached to my aunt and cousin when I got home.

He was calling my aunt's mom, and my cousin couldn't even leave out of his eyesight. Within those three months, they spoiled him. That let me know right then that he was in the best hands. I was grateful that they had taken him with them. They showed him unconditional love, and still, to this day, he calls my aunt mom.

He and my cousin have a love-hate relationship right now, but you can't tell her anything about him. I loved my child forever when I got home. That was one of the greatest feelings in the world. Being able to see his little smile brought me so much joy. The next day I went to see the guy's parents to thank them for everything they had done for me.

Having that talk with them, I discovered a lot of back-biting going on. Some family members had done some dirty spiteful things while I was in jail. It was a sad situation because you would think your family should have your back, not mine. For the most part, it's always been every man for themselves since I was growing up. I couldn't focus on what they had done because my main focus was on my child and getting back to where I needed to be.

Being home was a blessing, but reality had started to sink in. I was home, and I had absolutely nothing. I was right back to square one. No job, no house, no money, no nothing. One of the worse feelings in the world is to have worked so hard for something only to lose it all.

My aunt, who had my son, had her own life and kids, but she never denied my son and me a place to stay. She never turned me away when I got out. I stayed there with her for a few months, and every day I walked to go job searching.

I had a son who needed me; hell, I needed me too. I refused to allow my depression to sink in.

All my hard work in job searching had finally paid off. I got hired to work at O'Reilly's Auto Parts as a cashier and delivery driver. I knew nothing about car parts, but a job was a job. I knew someone was going to train me, so I took the position. My plans for my son and me required a job right down the street from the house.

I walked to and from work every day until I could get a car. The job didn't pay as much as I thought it would have, but it was enough to stay afloat for my son and me. I could take care of my son like I did before I went to jail, and that's all that mattered to me. Christmas was slowly approaching; my ex and I were no longer together, but I kept in contact with his parents. They loved my child and me, and we loved them.

He and I were just cordial. We weren't together for many reasons and being arrested and locked away from my son behind his bullshit was my deal breaker. My son and I got invited to his parent's house for Christmas, so we went. Little did I know, he had something up his sleeves. Everything felt like old times being over there.

Family and friends were there having a good time as usual. We laughed and talked about all kinds of things. Mid-conversation, he stopped and said he had something to say. Everyone became quiet to listen to him speak. He walked over to me, apologizing for everything he had done to me and what he had put me through.

He then dropped to one knee, asking me to marry him. I was lost for words, and my heart felt like it was going to beat out of my chest. I honestly didn't want to respond or make him look stupid in front of his family and friends, so I said yes. I knew in the back of my mind I couldn't marry him. I wasn't over all the hurt he caused me.

Not only that, but I also felt that he had only asked for my hand in marriage because his sister was engaged. After everyone saw the ring, hugged, and congratulated us, we continued to spend family time. I told him I needed time to think about everything and that he and I would sit down and talk. I returned to my aunt's house and showed them the ring, and they were happy about it, but I wasn't. My heart was still hurting deeply.

Come to think of it; he never came to visit me when I was in jail. He wasn't holding my son down as he had promised, and he was back in the streets cheating.

So, to me, that was the most disloyal thing he could ever do to me. I was done with him because I knew I deserved better. Once we had our conversation, I kept it real and told him how I felt and that I couldn't marry him.

I took the ring off to give it back to him, but he told me to keep it because I deserved it. That was one of the most heartbreaking conversations I ever had to have. It was indeed the end for us, but I knew I would be okay. My focus was on my child and striving to become better. I still needed to do more as I continued working.

I felt as if I needed to do more. The following year came around, and I was able to file my taxes. With that money, I was able to get a car. It wasn't a brand-new car with zero miles, but it was a car, one that I needed for my son and me, mainly to get back and forth to work. I was tired of walking and asking for a ride; in the back of my mind, that wasn't enough; I couldn't stop there.

One day, I was watching TV, and a commercial came on about Camelot Career College showing that they offered all types of programs, housing for students and their kids, financial aid, etc. That was like a blessing in disguise for me. I kept telling myself that was my change right there.

I needed to talk to someone from that school to see what it was all about. Being who I am, I didn't just think about myself; I also took my cousin and best friend to check the school out.

We all needed to further our education. After talking to the advisor at the school, I signed up the same day. Everything sounded good to me. It was a school where I could obtain another diploma. They had on-campus daycare and housing, so my son could always stay on campus with me.

All three of us were accepted into the school and were able to move onto campus the next day. I was super excited. We all returned home and shared the news. I thanked my aunt for all she had done for my son and me, but it was time that I stood back up on my own two feet and did what I needed for me and mine. She offered to keep my son at times while I went to school, and I allowed her because she had a bond with my son; that was also a big help to me.

My best friend and I moved to the campus within two-three days. We didn't know what we were getting ourselves into, but it was a new start for us, and I needed a fresh start away from everyone. The dorm rooms only had a bed and dresser, with one shelf to fold and hang clothes. That was all I needed; it was my own space.

Other women and their children stayed in different dorms, and it was amazing to see all the single mothers trying to make it.

Once I got used to being there, it was like my brain turned on a green switch. I linked up with some of the other women there, and we partied. Every single night I went to the club. I was drinking and smoking; I even popped a pill every once in a while, to help ease my mind. What I thought was over, I wasn't. All that hurt and pain came back all at once.

However, I didn't allow my partying lifestyle to cause me to flunk out of school; I made sure I went to class every day. My son was still going to my aunt, so I had plenty of time to do what I wanted. I didn't care what anyone thought because everyone there had a story to tell. We all were there for a reason, and some of our reasons were the same.

We needed somewhere to go. As time passed, I grew tired of doing the same thing and knew I had to get my shit together. It was either I swim or sink, and I damn sure didn't want to sink. I didn't go there to become a failure in life. I felt like I had already failed my son when I went to jail; I refused to fail him again.

It was now or never in my eyes. I decided to pull myself together and truly focus on changing who I was for the better. I started focusing on school, giving up the club life. While there, I met some amazing women. We made it through like family because, truth be told, for most of us, we were the only family we had.

It wasn't all peaches and cream, but we made the best out of every situation. When one cooked, we all ate. Everyone looked out for everyone, especially when it came down to our kids because we were all we had. Some of those women don't know how they help save me in many ways. I would tell anyone if you made it staying at Camelot, you are a strong individual.

That school helped save many of us; some don't even know it. While being there was still a struggle, I can confidently say I made it. I graduated with honors and a diploma in Medical Assisting. It was the start of something great for my son and me. All that I had been through, I had finally put behind me.

I was proud of myself and who I was becoming. Although everything seemed like it was falling apart, me going to jail, facing a ten-to-life charge, and losing everything I worked hard to build for my son and me, I never lost my faith in God. If I was never taught anything else, I was taught that God would fight all my battles.

He would and could bring me through any situation. I knew that he was my lawyer in the courtroom.

I knew who I served and how powerful he was. My favorite scriptures that kept me going and fighting daily were Philippians 4:13 and Psalms 91. It was knowing that I could do all things through Christ, who gives me strength. I was about to return to school and accomplish something greater for my son and me. One thing I know for sure is that my God is awesome.

Give yourself permission to revisit the relationships and connections that may have led you down the wrong path. Revisit those wounds that may have caused rage and anger to explode in your life and caused you to regret some of the decisions you made because of it. It is okay to forgive yourself and to move one. When everyone walks away from you during your hard times, God will be there to wipe those tears, lift your head, and give you all the strength you need to keep pushing. Make a decision to heal *OUTLOUD*!

CHAPTER 3

Love & Heartbreak

Shortly after my mother passed away, I found out the man I was deeply in love with cheated on me with a woman that he met in a club. Talk about a double whammy in the same month; I was numb. My world felt shattered, and it felt like I couldn't breathe. Before all that, let me take you down the path that led me to say, screw love to hell with life, for that matter!!! I will live my life how I want to, and I will do what I want to.

I want to tell you what pushed me into an "I don't give an f..... mindset!" Back in 2009, I met a man, and we instantly fell in love. He was a very charming, respectful, family-oriented, gentleman, homebody, leader, and a provider; you know, all the things we look for in a man. I was only twenty-three years old with a three-year-old son, and he was older than I was. When we met, I had just graduated as a Medical Assistant in Baton Rouge, LA.

I was ready to settle down and have a family because my time running the streets and partying was up. So, when I met him, I was prepared for the real world, a real man, and a family. It was like I met him at the right time in my life.

We began to date shortly after, and everything is going great. He loved my son, and my son loved being around him.

Three months into dating, he stated that he wanted to be with me and thought it would be best if my son and I moved in with him. We didn't live in the same city, so I would have to move out of my apartment and move in with him. At first, it seemed too good to be true, but then I was like, "the hell with it; why not give it a chance?" I kept replaying in my mind, *isn't this what you've been saying you wanted?* After about a week or two of going back and forth to decide whether I wanted to give up my own place to move in with him, I finally did.

I mean, after all, I did develop feelings for him. He was doing everything right. The day I moved in was a breeze, and he got me, and my son settled in quickly. My son was all for it. They developed a close bond that I believed would become unbreakable. He truly cared, and it showed. Months went by, and everything was fantastic.

He was everything and more that I wanted. I was in love with him and how he loved my son and me. Something about how that man made me feel as a woman drew me closer and closer to him: I loved him, and I just knew I was going to be his wife.

He had my nose wide open, and I didn't see anything wrong. Love is truly blind.

I admired our family time with our kids because it was always about making them happy. We both worked and took care of our family. It was just something about this man that I found too good to be true. I don't know whether it was the fact I had never had a man to show me authentic love -not even my father, but I could find no wrong in him. Don't get me wrong; things weren't all peaches and cream.

We had our typical little fusses and disagreements, but nothing major. You know the saying; you don't really know a person until you start living with them; boy, that shit is true. I don't know if it was because he was older than me, but everything seemed to get on his nerves. Two years into the relationship, I realized that he was what you call a narcissist. It started being his way or no way at all.

Not caring about how I felt, he became selfish and self-centered. He was becoming emotionless and indifferent. It was like we were really only becoming roommates. I was so crazy in love with him, so I overlooked all the signs trying to make it work. I even started changing who I was as a woman to satisfy him.

I thought I was the problem. I changed my look; he didn't like it. I tried to role-play and spice things up, but he didn't like it. I tried talking to him about it, but he wasn't trying to hear what I had to say. He brushed it off like nothing was ever wrong.

However, no matter what was on my mind, I would fight for my family. As time began to pass by, he started hanging out late, which was unusual because he was never the going-out type of man. He had never gone into a club while he and I were together; I didn't think he was hanging there, but I was wrong. He had gotten a taste of the streets all over again. We began to argue daily.

He picked arguments to get a reaction out of me. I grew tired, yet I was still hoping we could have fixed things because I thought this man was my soulmate, the man I knew I would marry one day. I knew I wanted to make it work and was determined to do so. I started to think about ways to rekindle our love and romance. Thinking about how I can get things back to when we first met.

I started buying new lingerie for a bit of role-playing in the bedroom. I even tried changing my hair to bring on a new look. Before I knew it, I was changing who I was to try to keep a man, something I'd never done, constantly saying things would get better.

Well, nothing had gotten better. We were growing apart daily, and it showed.

At this point, my heart kept tugging at the fact that he may have been cheating, but I didn't have any proof. I remember saying, "what's done in the dark will always come to light." I began to pray daily for whatever was to be revealed to me so that I could move on with my life, and that's just what happened. God started showing me all that I needed to know. One day, we had an intense argument because I decided to take my son to the zoo, and I didn't invite him or his daughter.

Honestly, I was at a place where I got tired of hearing the answer no to everything I had asked. I took it upon myself to have a mommy and son day. I never thought it would have come down to the point of us breaking up. There had to be more to it. I didn't dwell on the words he said that day; we both continued with our day like normal.

When I returned home that day, he was still gone— no big deal. I packed our bags and headed to Donaldsonville for the weekend to stay with my family, and we didn't talk at all that weekend. Once I returned home that Sunday afternoon, I told him we needed to talk about what had happened. He stated, "I don't have anything to talk about; it's over." I was like ok, cool.

I begin moving my things into the guest bedroom in silence. My heart was shattered, but I couldn't allow him to see me hurt. That night I cried myself to sleep, but I knew it was game time. The next day I began looking for a spot of my own, not knowing where I would move, but I knew I had to get out of that house from around him. He had changed, and I knew it wasn't about us.

My gut told me he was messing with another woman. One thing about it is when I start to get these gut-wrenching feelings about someone: I'm never wrong. Two weeks passed, and I was still in the guest room, trying to find a place. We were both at a place where we were now officially just roommates. We were both on the "do as you please and I will do the same" vibe.

I didn't care what he did because, once again, whatever he was doing would be revealed one way or another. A month passed, and I was still searching for somewhere to move. I hadn't had any luck with finding anything. It seemed like they were only taking applications to get on a waiting list. Then one day, I got a call asking if I still needed a place.

Without any hesitation, I said yes. The next day I went to go and look at the home, and it was not what I was used to. It didn't matter, though; it would be mine. I just needed to get out from around him.

Once I accepted the spot, I returned to the house and told him I had found a place and would be moving by the end of the month.

He must have thought I was joking about moving out; his whole facial expression changed. He couldn't have possibly thought I would stay there, and we weren't together. No way in hell was I going to continue to live there. It hurt me to my core, leaving what I helped build, but I knew it was for the better. When the time came for me to go, he was willing to help move me out.

Remember, I said that what's done in the dark shall come to light. That's precisely what happened. When the time came for me to leave and move out, something felt weird. It felt like something was going to happen, and I couldn't put my hands on it. When he got off work, I was packed up, ready to move out.

He went and showered first, so I laid down across the bed until he finished. While I waited, his phone went off. Checking his phone was something I had never done before; therefore, I ignored it. The phone went off again, but this time, I said what the hell, and I checked. What I saw crushed everything in me.

My gut wasn't wrong at all. His trifling ass was indeed cheating with another woman. It all made sense how all of a sudden, he had changed.

The message clearly stated that he loved her and would be together soon. That was it; I had lost my shit.

I kicked open the bathroom door, angry as hell. Screaming at him, asking, "how could you do this to me after all I've done for you." I was hurt, my soul was crushed, and my heart was broken into pieces. He was so nonchalant about everything. As we loaded the truck, I tried my hardest not to show my emotions because I was dying inside.

Once we got to my new apartment, we unloaded everything inside and said our goodbyes. Finally, I was in my own home. That night my emotions were all over the place. It was so uncomfortable; I was used to going home to him and the kids, but things were about to be different. I endured many restless nights, but I pushed through the daily hurt.

Time went by, and we didn't speak much at all. I lost my mom two and a half weeks after our breakup. Talk about one hard hit after another. That day I got the call about my mom; it felt like all the wind had left out of my body. As I traveled to Donaldsonville, I called him to tell him what had happened because she loved him to the fullest.

She wasn't aware of our breakup yet. I hadn't had a chance to tell her what had happened. She was my voice of reasoning, and I was hers. Once I told him about what happened to my mom, he was there every step of the way. He even attended the funeral with me as my support.

That was one of my most challenging moments, and I was happy to have him by my side. We weren't back together, but he was there. That opened up our lines of communication again. Before that, we weren't speaking at all. After the burial of my mom, things went back to normal.

We both continued to go on with our lives as before, expecting nothing from one another. We conversed through text messages off and on but nothing serious. Talking to him gave me a sense of calmness, though. Those messages landed us back down memory lane, and we discussed how much we had missed each other.

One day we ended up hooking up for a night of pleasure, and then it was on from there. That became our routine. He would come to see me, and I would also drive to see him. At the time, I wasn't thinking; I wanted him. Was he still involved with the other woman?

Yes! But I didn't care. In my mind, he was mine first, and I didn't give a damn about her feelings. She didn't care about mine, so I continued to be with him. We continued to see each other every weekend.

Our affair continued for years after the breakup. We weren't together, but he still took care of my household. He paid bills and bought gifts for birthdays and holidays. My son and I didn't want anything, and he was one call away, that's all. The sex seemed to be better than before, and I started to desire more from him.

I wanted what we should have had before he stepped out of our relationship. In the back of my mind, I knew he wasn't trying to leave either of us alone. He had the best of both worlds. We went at this for three years strong. I finally reached my breaking point with this man.

He wasn't trying to fix or better our situation; he was enjoying the benefits that came with me. Him and the chick he cheated on me with had moved in together, yet he was still playing house with me. When I realized that he was only dealing with me so that no one else could have me was the day I walked away. It was right before my birthday. I had decided that I was going to end it and move forward with my life.

I deserved more than I was allowing myself to have. I couldn't be mad because I gave him just that much willpower to think what we were doing was ok when it wasn't. Everything I did was on some get-back shit towards her, but in the end, all I was really doing was hurting myself. I made sure she knew everything before I walked away from him. I remember telling her that payback was a bitch and that she could finally have her man all to herself because I was done with him.

Walking away was one of the best feelings in the world. I started doing what was best for me and made me happy. I started living my life for myself all over again. Finding love was the last thing on my mind. I just wanted to be free, and finally I was.

I knew that one day love would come, but until then, I just wanted to live my life to the fullest; that's precisely what I did. You will do anything for love when you're lost, broken, and vulnerable searching for love in all the wrong places. Instead of finding love within myself, I looked to others to help give me a temporary fix. I was lost, and I didn't even know it. However, I found myself, and that is what matters the most. Love is supposed to heal and build you, not kill you. I started to heal out loud, and I never stopped.

CHAPTER 4

Losing You

Losing a parent is a hard pill for any child to swallow. It never becomes easy, but losing your mother is an unexplainable feeling. Whether it is your father or your mother, the pain cuts deep. For me, it was my mother, who was my very first best friend. She was the one I trusted with my entire life, the good and the bad.

She was my hiding place and the person I shared a very special bond with. Your mother is the person you desire, never to miss any special moments in your life. She's supposed to be your secret keeper, the one who nurtures you until she is too old to do it anymore. I lost this person, and my heart has never been the same. She was not perfect, but she was my mother, and that's all that matters.

Without her, there would've never been me. I have always been attached to her, even when we were apart. I wanted to be with her through the good, bad, and ugly. She struggled with drug addiction, but that never stopped me from loving her. She was still my everything.

In my eyes, she was the strongest woman that I knew. I never wanted to leave her in this cold world alone. I hoped I could have saved her, but that's not how life works. Sometimes, things that happen in peoples' lives are uncontrollable. I was mentally scarred when my mother left me physically to live with my grandmother but to lose her to death is beyond explanation.

It was never anything I could've ever prepared for. Her death was never a moment that I awaited. April 24, 2011, Easter Sunday, will be a day I won't ever forget. Like any other ordinary day, I got dressed for work. I signed up to do a double shift, so I would miss the family gatherings I planned to attend the month prior. It was common for me to work doubles, so it didn't bother me at all.

I started my day as usual and headed to work. My mother called me as she usually did every morning, but I couldn't take the call at the time. Unfortunately, I was with a patient. She must have called me three times back-to-back; I still didn't answer. When I didn't answer the last time, she left me a voicemail saying, "Hey, momma baby, I was calling to tell you that my grandson's Easter basket will be left by my sister's house; don't forget to come to pick my baby basket up."

I planned to call her back when I had free time, but I didn't. There was no reason I didn't call her back; I always did. However, on this day, I continued to work my long shift and didn't make the call back a priority, especially after hearing her voicemail.

I knew she loved me and wanted to see how I was doing, and most importantly, she wanted me to pick up my baby's Easter basket. My best friend and I planned to go out that night, so I went to the mall on my lunch break to find something to wear.

I couldn't find anything, so I told my friend that it was a sign that we needed to stay home. There was too much indication that we didn't need to go; something seemed off. I just shook it off and went back to work. After about an hour or so passed, I received a phone call from one of my cousins telling me that I needed to rush home because something had happened to my mom. That conversation felt unreal; I didn't believe it, so I immediately hung up the phone.

Anyone who knows my family knows they are childish and play all day, so I didn't take the call seriously at all. Even though I heard this loud commotion in the background, I overlooked that something could've actually be wrong.

About two-three minutes later, my phone rang again; but that time, my grandmother told me she needed me to get home but to drive carefully. She told me she would explain everything once I made it over there. My heart immediately started to skip beats.

I recall being so numb that I couldn't respond, so the nurse on duty took my phone from me to finish the conversation with my grandmother. In my mind, I was still trying to register what could have suddenly happened to my mother. She seemed okay that morning when she left the voicemail, so I didn't understand what was happening. It seemed like forever waiting for my best friend to make it to my job to pick me up. While waiting on my ride, my Facebook page instantly began to alert me with notifications with people commenting on a picture.

I didn't know which picture it was until I opened it up. My face instantly began to get hot. I felt like I was really about to pass out. The tears started flowing because I couldn't believe what I saw. Up and down my timeline, all I saw was "RIP" and "you will be missed."

I was livid, thinking to myself, is this really real? I remember feeling like I would pass out after seeing all the RIP posts about my mother. My emotions were all over the place.

I didn't know if what I was reading was real or not because my family hadn't confirmed anything. They never told me that she had passed away.

As we drove to Donaldsonville, all I kept saying to myself was Lord, please give me the strength to deal with whatever I am about to walk into. I knew I needed God to go ahead of me because I was too afraid to walk into that situation alone. We continued to drive for what seemed like forever. The closer we got, the more I felt like I wanted to vomit. My mind kept telling me that she was still alive, but something in my spirit kept saying she was gone.

I was in between; help me, Lord, and everything is okay. I could hear his soft whispers saying, "You're strong enough to get through this. She is no longer suffering. She's at peace now and needs you to be okay to do what needs to be done." Once we got to the corner of the street where the hospital was located, my nerves were in my stomach.

My emotions were high; I was trying to keep myself together. The streetlights seemed brighter than ever before, and cars were all up and down the road. When we pulled up, people were everywhere. I remember seeing my family from afar, crying and hugging each other, and that's when I lost it.

My friend was trying to find a parking spot, but I was ready to jump out of the moving car because all I wanted to see was my mother.

I just wanted to know if she was okay and if she needed me to help her out of that bed. As I got out of the car, my sisters and cousins tried to meet me halfway. All I wanted to know was that my mom was okay and that what I saw on FB wasn't true. My sister cried hysterically, screaming, and saying, "momma gone, sis, momma gone." My whole body felt numb, and I was angry!

I needed to know what had happened. All I knew was that she had been hit by a car. But was it a drunk driver? What could have possibly gone wrong to cause my mother to die? Did they not see her?

What caused this accident? I needed answers before I blew up on everybody! As I walked into the hospital, my mind was blank. It was like I didn't see anyone. I really wanted to see my mother before the coroner came to get her, but they told me that the doctor recommended that I not see her.

It was best to remember her the way she was; all I could do was cry. It finally hit me that my mother, my very first best friend, was dead. She wasn't coming back. We patiently waited for the coroner to come and get her body.

I may have paced back and forth a million times, trying to make sense of it all.

I was taught never to question God and that he doesn't make mistakes, but I had a lot of questions I needed him to answer for me. My mother had been on drugs for as long as I could remember, and I honestly thought drugs would be the cause of her death. I never imagined that she would have left us due to a tragic accident. It was unbelievable and still is today. At the tender age of twenty-five, I was burying my mother!

To me, life wasn't fair at all. I was so upset with God! How much did he think I could take in one month? The guy I thought I would spend the rest of my life with was no longer my significant other. Our breakup was very fresh, and I was starting to work towards healing from that breakup; now, my mother was dead.

I couldn't call him to be my shoulder to cry on; I was all over the place with everything. My siblings were all emotionally broken, and we couldn't picture life without her not being around anymore. For the longest time, I thought that maybe if I had answered my phone that morning, she would have stayed home. I wondered if she was actually trying to tell me something that morning before her death. I DON'T KNOW!!!

But I used to beat myself up all the time, wishing I could have answered her call. I couldn't get another chance to hear her voice again. Losing her broke me in so many ways I didn't even think it was possible. My heart was shattered. I felt like I was robbed of more time with her, but I also knew in my heart that she was tired of living in this cruel world.

She had spoken to me about it many times before. She knew there was healing, deliverance, and peace from the troubles of this world on the other side. For years I've tried to deal with the thought that time heals all wounds, but I'll be honest, it doesn't. Truth be told, I never had a chance to grieve; I am just starting to mourn. As the years passed by, I grieved for my mother even more.

When it came down to planning my mother's burial, I had to put my big girl panties on to handle business. That was one of the hardest things I had to do in my entire life, and I think that's why God allowed me to be at work at the time of the accident. I know that I wouldn't have been able to handle doing anything. Her not being here is something that I am still learning how to deal with. There are things that I wish she were here to see and share with her, but I never had the chance to.

There were so many conversations we needed to have. I believe God gave his most challenging battles to his strongest soldiers, which was what my mom was. She had the voice of an angel. Everyone loved to hear her sing. That voice of hers would break you down into tears.

She stood strong and firm no matter how hard things may have gotten. I'll forever cherish our bittersweet memories and carry them in my heart. I will never forget all of the things she taught me directly and indirectly. She was always my favorite lady! My mom, my angel, my everything, until we meet again, continue to rest in heaven; I love you.

CHAPTER 5

*Healing **Outloud***

When you have lived a life that has been full of brokenness, obstacles, and trials, you become numb to the world around you. You begin to lose sight of yourself, self-hatred can start settling in, and you may give up! You smile to keep from crying when it feels like you're slowly dying inside—no longer recognizing yourself. Some people begin to self-medicate with alcohol, drugs, sex, etc., to numb the pain because it makes life easier without worries. If you feel this way, know that you are not alone and can get through this season of your life.

You must decide to live past and beyond what happened to you and create a new narrative. There was a point where all my past situations hindered me from what I deserved. I felt unworthy of life and love, so I settled for what I thought was really love and happiness. The world weighed me down on my shoulders while trying to figure out who I truly was. I used to wonder what my purpose here on this earth was.

People didn't know the hurt, betrayal, depression, or suicidal thoughts that clouded my mind on many occasions but leaving my son alone in this cold world reminded me why I should live. I didn't have my mother to raise me; I didn't want to leave my son to struggle as I did. He was the only thing that honestly kept me striving to do better. I knew he looked up to me; I was all he had. So, I continued to press forward every day.

I woke up daily, reminding myself that somebody depended on me to live. Every day I pretended to be ok, but I wasn't. All my life, I've been the go-to person; they've always seen me as the strong one, but deep down inside, I was broken, hurt, and trying to heal simultaneously. No one ever saw me broken.

I've always worn a smile on my face regardless of what I was going through. I learned how to cope with whatever I was dealing with in the dark. For years, I didn't trust people around me and my children. Sometimes, I still find myself backing up from those who may get too close to me. Being broken and bitter from past hurt caused me to be mean and hateful toward people that really cared about me.

I truly believed that people were out to hurt me when they could have been there to help me. I allowed myself to pretend that I was ok when I wasn't, searching for love in all the wrong places because all I've ever wanted was to be loved by any means necessary. I didn't realize that what I needed to do, indeed, was to learn how to love myself truly. I knew that to love myself whole-heartedly, I needed to release myself of all the old soul ties, family hurt, and betrayal. Most of all, I had to learn to forgive myself and those who caused me harm.

Breaking my silence was the best thing I decided to do because it allowed me to heal and love myself-releasing and letting go; I finally know what love feels like within. I'm allowing myself to HEAL *OUTLOUD*! I chose to heal *OUTLOUD* because I've been silent for most of my life. I've held things inside that broke me into pieces for years. I've dwelled on not having anyone to turn to about the things I was dealing with, and most of the secrets I held to myself were because of all the stories I heard growing up from family arguments.

I knew no one would believe me if I opened my mouth. So many family secrets were swept under the rug; mine would have been one added to the hiding place. However, I am not my family's secret, and won't be silent anymore.

In true healing, you begin to allow the roads to your new journey to guide you to your destiny. The roads you must travel on aren't easy, but you can get along them.

I finally decided to let my roads lead me. They weren't comfortable or easy, it wasn't easy, but it was worth it. One of my biggest struggles with healing was forgiving the people who hurt me. Forgiving my molesters and those who treated me like I was nothing was hard. Each day I battled with the decision of whether I wanted to forgive them for the pain that they caused.

Some days my mind said yes, and there were days when my heart said no. Deep down inside, I knew that in order to get the healing and closure I needed, I had to forgive. During my healing journey, I began to drift back into depression. There were days when I would cry while writing because I was allowing my mind to get the best of me. Sometimes, I didn't even want to finish writing this book.

I was too afraid to tell my truth because I was worried about what people would say about me. I began to get discouraged with everything, ready to throw in the towel. The more I wrote, the more I became angry all over again. I knew I wouldn't get through writing this book if I continued to be frustrated and angry. Something had to change.

I took a break from writing to have a serious one-on-one with God to express how I felt about everything. I honestly had to go into a place where I began to fast and pray, asking God to direct my path as I told my story. Speaking daily affirmations over my life became my new normal. That was something that helped me through the struggle of writing and releasing. God began to show up and show out.

Sometimes, God will break you down to where you can only depend upon him. He will break you down to absolutely nothing. Once I allowed God to have his way in my life, things started to change. He started detaching me from people and places that no longer held a purpose in my life. The place I used to go and the things I used to do no were no longer my desire.

My hunger for God was activated in full force. It became lonely on this journey, but all the things I had been praying for were coming to pass. God was healing and revealing. He was indeed working on my behalf. I was where I needed to be for my healing to begin.

Most people won't understand that when you surrender your all to heal, the devil will throw curve balls in to throw you off track. I learned how to stand firm throughout this journey to heal.

My walk with Christ is nowhere near perfect, but I know God has a purpose for my life. I've known this since I was a young girl. Sometimes in life, you must go through rainy days to see the sunshine, and that's ok.

Life isn't a fairy tale nor perfect, but once you allow God to enter the midst of it, it can be better than you ever imagined. One thing I know for sure is that I am worthy of living. I have a purpose here on this earth. I kept faith in the size of a mustard seed and watered it daily with my prayers and worship. Therefore, I can firmly declare that God has destined me for greatness, love, happiness, financial wealth, a closer walk with Him, and all the desires of my heart.

I AM FREE!

I AM A GENERATIONAL CURSE BREAKER!

I AM HEALING OUT LOUD AND NO LONGER BROKEN & SO CAN YOU!

-Deliza Phillip

Made in the USA
Columbia, SC
28 July 2024

38976092R00055